KINGFISHER
An imprint of Larousse plc
Elsley House, 24–30 Great Titchfield Street,
London W1P 7AD

First published by Kingfisher 1994
2 4 6 8 10 9 7 5 3 1

ISBN 1 85697 240 2

Series editor: Sue Nicholson
Editor: Brigid Avison
Assistant editor: Sara Grisewood
Cover design: Terry Woodley
Design: Ben White Associates
Cover illustrations: Ann Winterbotham
Ann Winterbotham's illustrations previously published
in *All About Farm Animals* Kingfisher 1988
Illustrations on pp 17 & 23 by Maggie Brand
(Maggie Mundy Agency)
Typeset by SPAN, Lingfield, Surrey
Printed in Great Britain by BPC Paulton Books Limited

Farm Animals

Brenda Cook

Illustrated by Ann Winterbotham

Kingfisher

Contents

Early morning   7
Milking time   8
Back to the field   10
Farm babies   12
Sheep and lambs   14
Woolly fleeces   16
Pigs and piglets   18
Whose house?   20
Poultry and eggs   22
Caring for animals   24
In the winter   26
Some special words   28
Index   29

Early morning

Early in the morning when most of us are still fast asleep in bed, the farmer is out in the farmyard getting ready for another busy day. The farm animals wake up early too, and they all need to be fed and cared for.

Farmers have to work at all times of day.

The cock crows as a new day begins.

Milking time

Farmers keep cows for their meat or their milk. Cows are milked twice a day – early in the morning and late in the afternoon.

The cows eat their breakfast while the milking machine gently pumps the milk from their udders.

Every day, a big tanker collects the milk from the farm. The driver calls at several other farms, too. When the tank is full, it is taken to the milk factory.

The milk is pumped into a huge fridge.

Back to the field

After the morning milking, the cows are taken back to the field. A cow needs to have a baby before she starts making milk. After her calf is born she can give the farmer milk for almost a year.

Cows live in groups called herds.

At the milk factory, milk is made into many kinds of food, such as butter, cheese, yoghurt, and ice-cream. Food made from milk is called dairy food.

The gate is shut to keep the cows in the field.

Farm babies

Many baby animals are born in the springtime, so spring is a busy time on the farm. Some farm animals, such as horses, have just one baby at a time. Others, like cats, have lots of babies.

Do you know the names of the farm babies in these pictures?

1 Baby cows

2 Baby hens

3 Baby sheep

4 Baby goats

5 Baby ducks

6 Baby pigs

Sheep and lambs

Sheep live outdoors for most of the year. All day long, they nibble away at the grass. If the grass gets too short, the sheep are moved to a new field. When the farmer needs to move the sheep, the sheepdogs help to round them up.

The farmer whistles and calls to the sheepdog, so it knows what to do.

A newborn lamb can't eat grass. At first, it can only feed on its mother's milk. If the mother sheep dies, the farmer needs to keep the lamb warm and feed it from a bottle, like a human baby.

Woolly fleeces

In cold weather, sheep grow thick
woolly coats called fleeces. In
summer, the farmer shears them.

Electric clippers
are used to cut
the fleece.

The woolly fleece
comes off in one
huge piece.

Shearing is a bit like having a
short haircut! It doesn't hurt the
sheep at all.

MAKE A WOOLLY SHEEP

All you need to make this collage is some paper, poster paints, glue and plenty of cotton wool.

1 Draw a simple outline of a sheep on a large sheet of paper.

2 Paint the sheep's face and legs. You could glue on yellow buttons for the sheep's eyes.

3 Spread glue over the sheep's body and press torn up cotton wool on to it to make the sheep's white fluffy coat.

Pigs and piglets

Some farmers keep only one kind
of animal, such as pigs. Many
pigs live inside all year round, but
some live outdoors in huts.

A sow has about 12 piglets at a time.

A mother pig is called a sow.
When the sow is ready to have her
piglets, she's moved to a farrowing
pen. The piglets must not get cold
so the farmer hangs a special
lamp over them. The tiny piglets
sleep under its warm light.

Whose house?

Most farms have lots of buildings. Some of them are used to keep the animals safe and warm during the night or in winter. Can you match these animals to their houses?

Cow

Sheep

Dog

Chicken

Horse

Duck

ANSWERS

1 Barn for sheep
2 Stable for horses
3 Shed for ducks
4 Cowshed for cows
5 Kennel for dogs
6 Henhouse for chickens

21

Poultry and eggs

Hens are a kind of poultry, and so are ducks and geese. They all lay eggs that are good to eat but most people eat hens' eggs.

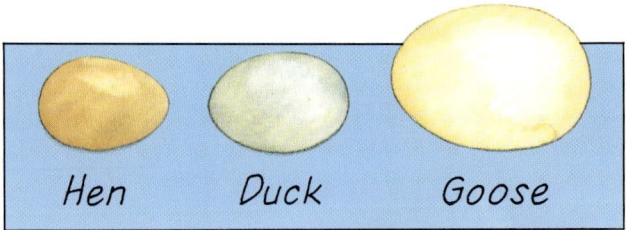

| Hen | Duck | Goose |

Ducks find food under water.

Geese eat weeds and grass.

MAKE AN EGG-HEAD

Next time you have eggs for breakfast save one of the eggshells to make a head with growing hair.

1 Put some damp cotton wool in the shell and cover it with lots of cress or alfalfa seeds.

2 Paint a face on the egg then wait a few days for the hair to grow.

Hens get fed each day with cereals and kitchen scraps.

Caring for animals

If an animal is ill or hurt the farmer asks the vet to visit the farm. Sometimes the vet will give the animals injections to keep them healthy and strong.

Sheep don't like injections any more than we do!

△ The vet uses a stethoscope to check the cow's insides. The farmer strokes the cow's head to keep it calm.

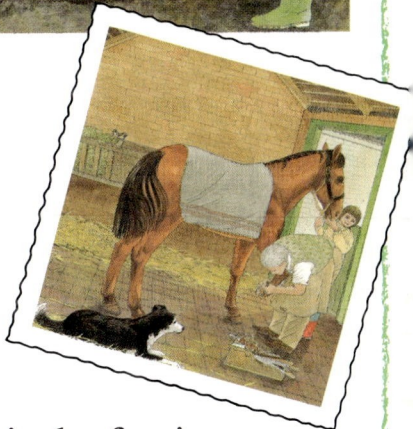

Another visitor is the farrier. Horses need shoes made of iron to protect their hooves from hard ground. The farrier nails on new horseshoes when the old ones wear out. It doesn't hurt the horse.

In the winter

When winter comes, the farmer
brings the cows into the cowshed,
out of the cold. They go back to
the fields in the spring when the
weather gets warmer.

In very cold weather, the farmer may bring the sheep indoors, too. The sheep and cows are fed on hay.

The farmer feeds the animals every day.

Some special words

Farrier Someone who makes and fits new horseshoes.

Farrowing pen A special pen where a sow is taken to have her piglets.

Poultry Hens, ducks, geese, turkeys and other farmyard birds.

Shearing Cutting off a sheep's fleece, usually with electric shears. The fleece is then sent off to make wool.

Vet Short for **veterinary**. A doctor for sick animals.

Index

calf   10, 12–13

chicken   12, 22–23

cow   8–9, 10–11

duck   13, 22

farrier   25

fleece   16

goose   22

hen   12, 22, 23

lamb   13, 15

milk   9, 8–9, 10–11

milking machine   8–9

pig   13, 18–19

poultry   22–23

sheep   13, 14, 16–17

sheepdog   14

sheep shearing   16

vet   24–25

wool   16–17